Hast

TROLLEYBUSES

Lyndon W Rowe
Series editor Robert J Harley

MP **Middleton Press**

Cover Picture: Passengers alight on to the seafront at White Rock. This trolleybus, Sunbeam built 31, is on the long coastal route from Alexandra Park to Cooden and has come from the Memorial via Robertson Street. The atmosphere of a seaside town is conveyed by the coloured lights strung from the lamp standard to the right of the vehicle. (C. Carter)

Published August 1996

Reprinted April 1999

ISBN 1 873793 81 2

© Middleton Press, 1996

Design - Deborah Goodridge

Published by Middleton Press
        Easebourne Lane
        Midhurst
        West Sussex
        GU29 9AZ
        Tel: 01730 813169
        Fax: 01730 812601

Printed & bound by Biddles Ltd.
        Guildford and King's Lynn

CONTENTS

Opening Day	1	Alexandra Park to Memorial	48
Memorial Clock Tower	2	Ore to Clive Vale and Fishmarket	53
Memorial to Silverhill (via Bohemia)	6	Fishmarket to Memorial	65
Silverhill Depot	13	Hastings Station Loop	70
Hollington	16	Memorial to Silverhill (via Seafront)	74
Silverhill to St.Helens (via Baldslow)	23	Grand Parade to Bulverhythe Depot	84
St.Helens to Ore	31	Bulverhythe to Bexhill	90
Old London Road	40	Bexhill to Cooden Beach	99
Mount Road to Park Gates	43	Rolling Stock and Preserved Vehicles	103
Blacklands Loop	46	Finale - Replacement by Buses	116

INTRODUCTION AND ACKNOWLEDGEMENTS

It is true to say that most people always retain a special affection for the area where they were born and I am therefore particularly pleased to have the opportunity to provide this pictorial history of trolleybuses in the town and surrounding areas of Hastings. I have even been able to include a photograph of a trolleybus passing my birthplace which, although served by Hastings Tramways, was actually on the very fringe of the Hastings County Borough area. Perhaps it was the shadow of the trolley booms across the bedroom ceiling, as a Guy single decker passed on the infrequent Circular route, that gave me a love for the system and eventually ensured that I was present on the very last trolleybus to pass that spot on 31st May 1959. A sad day indeed.

Although my family moved away to North Kent soon after the start of World War 2, my grandparents remained in Hollington and frequent visits gave me a chance to get well acquainted with the trolleybuses and operations of the Hastings Tramways Company. I trust you will find these faithfully recorded in this book and hopefully it will bring back happy memories for all those who knew the system in its heyday.

I have assembled a comprehensive collection of photographs, covering the life of the system from the early days of Hastings & District, through the long period of operation by the Hastings Tramways Company, under the overall ownership of Maidstone & District Motor Services Ltd. and ending with the eventual absorption by M & D and conversion to buses. This book is not a detailed history, however, and covers the system on a geographical basis, rather than dealing with the operational aspects or with the debates that arose from time to time between the local councils and the company.

Some points should be borne in mind when following the pages of this book. Firstly, the availability of early material is not great and there is therefore a bias in the photography towards the later years of the system. Secondly, the replacement of the large single deck fleet by new double deck vehicles was commenced in 1940 and that was hardly a time for photographers to be about in a front line seaside town, especially with the imminent risk of invasion by enemy forces from across the Channel. Thirdly, the structure of the routes changed frequently during the 1930s, twelve route numbers being in use throughout most of this period. After the war, the structure stabilised and four numbers only were used until closure in 1959. For this reason, I have referred in some captions to the post-war route numbers along a stretch of road, rather than to the complex structure of earlier days, when many different route numbers may have served the same location.

Choosing the best way to tour the system was far from easy, as the services in the Hastings area did not follow wires dedicated solely to individual routes. I therefore decided to commence the survey at the Memorial and have generally followed trunk sections of wiring, diverting on occasions to fill in adjoining sections of route, whilst in the appropriate area of the town.

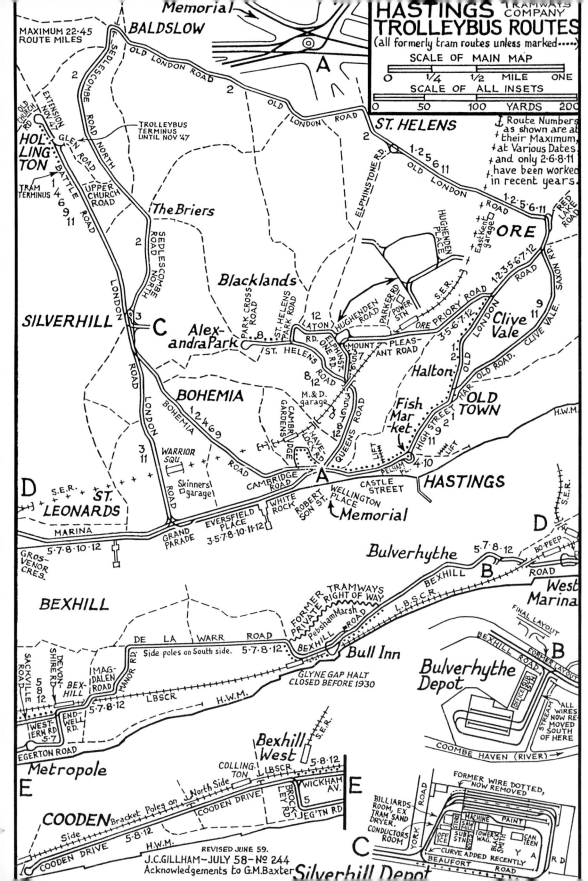

HASTINGS TRAMWAYS COMPANY
TROLLEYBUS ROUTES
(all formerly tram routes unless marked ·····)

SCALE OF MAIN MAP
0   1/4   1/2 MILE   ONE
SCALE OF ALL INSETS
0   50   100   YARDS   200

Route Numbers
as shown are at
their Maximum,
at Various Dates
and only 2·6·8·11
have been worked
in recent years.

MAXIMUM 22·45
ROUTE MILES

Memorial

BALDSLOW

OLD LONDON ROAD

A

St. HELENS

TROLLEYBUS
TERMINUS
UNTIL NOV '47

OLD LONDON ROAD

SEDLESCOMBE ROAD NORTH

HOL
LING
TON

OLD
CHURCH
RD.

EXTENSION
NOV. '47

GLEN ROAD

UPPER
CHURCH
ROAD

BATTLE ROAD

TRAM
TERMINUS

The Briers

1·2·5·6·11

ELPHINSTONE RD.

1·2·5·6·11
ROAD

Eastern
garage

ORE

RED
LAKE
ROAD

HUGHENDEN PLACE

1·2·3·5·6·7·12

SEDLESCOMBE ROAD NORTH

2

Blacklands

PARK CROSS ROAD

St. HELENS PARK ROAD

12
(LATON)
RD.

HUGHENDEN
ROAD

PARKER RD.
POWER
STN

S.E.R.

ORE

PRIORY ROAD

LONDON ROAD

SAXON RD.

Clive
Vale

9

11

SILVERHILL

3

C

Alex-
andra Park

St. HELENS ROAD

ST. HELENS ONE RD.

ELPHINST.
RD

3·5·6·7·12

1
2

OLD ROAD

CLIVE VALE

8

1·2·4·6·9

Halton

OLD TOWN

H.W.M.

London ROAD

BOHEMIA

1 2 4 6 9

Cambridge
Gardens

M. & D.
garage

Mount PLEAS-
ANT ROAD

Fish
Mar-
ket

9 2 1

LIFT

HIGH STREET

PELHAM RD.

LIFT

4·10

11

HASTINGS

3
11

WARRIOR
SQU.

CAMBRIDGE ROAD

HAVE-
LOCK RD.

QUEENS ROAD

Skinners
garage

12

A

CASTLE
STREET

D

S.E.R.

ST.
LEONARDS

MARINA

GRAND
PARADE

EVERSFIELD
PLACE
3·5·7·8·10·11·12

WHITE
ROCK

ROBERT
SON ST.

WELLINGTON
PLACE

Memorial

D

S.E.R.

5·7·8·10·12

GROS-
VENOR
CRES.

Bulverhythe

BEXHILL ROAD

5·7·8·12

L.B.S.C.R.

B

BO-PEEP
ROAD

West
Marina

FINAL LAYOUT

B

BEXHILL

DE LA WARR ROAD

FORMER TRAMWAYS
PRIVATE RIGHT OF WAY

Pebsham Marsh

BEXHILL ROAD

Bull Inn

Bulverhythe
Depot

BEXHILL ROAD FORMER LAYOUT

POLICE STN.

ALL
WIRES
NOW RE-
MOVED
SOUTH
OF HERE

Side poles on South side.   5·7·8·12

SACKVILLE
ROAD

DEVON-
SHIRE RD.

MAG-
DALEN
ROAD

MANOR RD.

BEX-
HILL

L.B.S.C.R.

H.W.M.

5·7·8·12

GLYNE GAP HALT
CLOSED BEFORE 1930

COOMBE HAVEN (RIVER)

5·8
12

END-
WELL
RD.

WEST-
ERN RD.
5·7

EGERTON ROAD

S.E.R.

Bexhill
West

5·8·12

FORMER WIRE DOTTED,
NOW REMOVED

Metropole

COLLING-
TON

North Side

L.B.S.C.R.

5·8·12

WICKHAM
AV.

BROCK-
LEY RD.

EG'TN RD.

5

BILLIARDS
ROOM, EX
TRAM SAND
DRYER

ROAD

YORK ROAD

MACHINE
SAW

PAINT

SUB
STN

TOWER
WAG.

CAN
TEEN

CONDUCTORS
ROOM

OFF-
ICE

BLACK-
SMITH

Y
A

BEAUFORT ROAD

CURVE ADDED
RECENTLY

E

COODEN

Bracket Poles on
North Side

COODEN DRIVE

Side

COODEN DRIVE   5·8·12

H.W.M.

REVISED JUNE 59.
J.C.GILLHAM~JULY 58~№ 244
Acknowledgements to G.M.Baxter

Silverhill Depot

C

A large number of photographs in this book come from my own camera but I am pleased to acknowledge the work of others whose photographs are included. Where known to me, credit is given but I have acquired many prints over the years that carry no indication of their origin and I hope that any one seeing his work in print but acknowledged only to my own collection will understand how this came about.

I would like to thank Robert Harley for giving me the opportunity to produce this book.

Thanks also to Hugh Taylor, David C. Padgham and Bob Cook for their great help in providing some of the photographs, as well as willingly loaning historical material. I also acknowledge the assistance of John Gillham for supplying the system map and I am indebted to Terry Russell for the rolling stock drawings. The *Maidstone & District Illustrated Fleet History 1911-1995*, published by the M & D and East Kent Bus Club in 1995, has also been a valuable source of reference.

GEOGRAPHICAL SETTING

Hastings and the neighbouring resorts of St. Leonards and Bexhill are located on the south coast of England in the county of East Sussex and some 60 miles/96 kms south east of London. The ground behind Hastings rises steeply, in places reaching heights of more than 500 feet/150 metres above sea level. The old town lies in a defile between the East and West Hills which stretch away from the coast to form the central Sandstone uplands of the Weald.

Towards Bexhill, a further dip exists in the hills at Glyne Gap whilst the extremity of the system at Cooden was on the eastern boundary of the Pevensey Levels.

HISTORICAL BACKGROUND

The history of Hastings and of the trams that preceded the trolleybuses has already been covered in *Hastings Tramways* published in 1993 as part of the *Tramway Classics* series. Suffice it here to say that Hastings is well known for the events of 14th October 1066 when the famous battle took place at Senlac field between King Harold and William of Normandy. The site of the conflict was actually some five miles inland at the location now known as Battle but Hastings has gained the historical benefit over the years from its position as the nearest settlement in those early days.

Hastings later became the premier Cinque Port and had close associations with the sea and the fishing industry, becoming a favourite seaside watering-place and resort after the arrival of the London, Brighton & South Coast and South Eastern Railways in 1851. The town is dominated by the ruins of the castle, built soon after 1066 but also has many other places of interest such as St.Clements Caves, the 15th Century church of All Saints and the extensive Alexandra Park. There are also two funiculars,

both still serving the public and each possessing different operational features. Although light industry developed later, summer visitors were the mainstay of the economy in Hastings and St.Leonards throughout the trolleybus era. Bexhill, some five miles to the west, is also a seaside town and a place much favoured by retired people. It was the scene of an early seaplane passenger service in 1919 but is nowadays largely residential. Bexhill was principally a seaside resort during the trolleybus era, although perhaps of a more genteel nature than its close neighbour Hastings, which was invaded in summer by day trippers.

Trolleybus operation in Hastings began on 1st April 1928, when route 4 commenced between Hollington and the Fishmarket via Bohemia Road. The section between the Memorial and the Fishmarket had not been served by the trams and thus saw wiring for the first time. Four gaily decorated vehicles inaugurated the service and an eight minute frequency was then operated throughout the day. On 21st May, the Silverhill - London Road -

Grand Parade - Memorial tramway was converted and on 30th July the sections between Alexandra Park and the Memorial and between Grand Parade (London Road) and West Marina (Bo-peep) became trolleybus operated. Bexhill first saw new vehicles on 18th September, when trolleybuses were extended from West Marina to Cooden, the reserved track tramway across Pebsham Marsh being replaced by wiring along Bexhill Road. Bulverhythe Depot now supplied vehicles for the coastal route.

The year 1929 saw the end of tramway operation. On 24th January, the Laton Road - Priory Road - Ore - St. Helens section was converted, whilst on 4th March, new wiring came into use from the Fishmarket to the Old Market Cross and over the tram route thence to Ore via Clive Vale. The extension through the narrow High Street was initially authorised for operation in one direction only at any one time, opposing vehicles having to operate via Mount Pleasant when the restrictions were in force. The final tram ran on 15th May 1929 when the Circular was converted on the remaining rural section between St.Helens and Silverhill.

The conversions had resulted in two slight extensions of wiring beyond the former tram termini, the first being a distance of 10 chains to reach the Victoria Inn reverser at Hollington, Glen Road and the second from the former tram terminus at Alexandra Park, St.Helens Park Road, to a new turning circle at Park Cross Road. Both extensions took place without the requisite powers being obtained; they were granted subsequently by an Act of 10th July 1930 which also authorised four new sections of wiring. These were Park Gates to the Langham via Elphinstone Road, opened on 10th August 1930, the Hastings Station loop, opened on 18th January 1931, the direct route through Bexhill via Western Road, opened on 1st July 1931 and some wiring along Hughenden Road, Langham, which was never erected.

The completion of these extensions brought the system to a length of 22 miles and 20 chains and marked the full extent of the wiring, apart from 300 yards erected in Hollington in 1947, when the reverser at Glen Road was replaced by a turning circle. Virtually all wiring, apart from that in Bulverhythe depot, was still in place at the closure in 1959. Fifty-eight new trolleybuses were introduced to service, eight open top and fifty single deck Guys; full details are given in the section on rolling stock. They were in the maroon and cream livery of the Hastings & District Tramways Company Ltd. and it is interesting to note that the double-deckers formed the first open top trolleybus fleet in the country, being approved in the first instance by the Ministry of Transport for an experimental period of six months. The routes changed frequently in the early days and timetables were not issued. As a guide, however, the position in 1932, by which time timetables did exist, was as follows:

Routes and service frequency (minutes)

1	Circular (via Queen's Road and St.Helens)	45
2	Circular (via St. Helens and Old London Road)	45
3	Hollington - Alexandra Park (via London Road)	10
4	Hollington - Fishmarket (via Bohemia Road)	7
5	Ore - Cooden (via Mount Pleasant)	20
6	Langham - West Marina	10
7	St.Helens - Bexhill (via Mount Pleasant)	20
8	Silverhill - West Marina (Summer only)	30
9	Hastings Station - Ore (via Clive Vale)	20
10	Hastings Station - Ore (via Old London Road)	20
11	Hollington - Ore (via London Road and Clive Vale)	10
12	Hollington - Mt.Pleasant Church (via London Road and Laton Road)	20

Services 5, 6 and 7 were worked from Bulverhythe depot, which housed 23 of the 58 vehicles. The eight open top Guys were employed on route 4 and on the coastal service. The maximum fare at this time was 9d (approx.4p).

On 11th November 1935, the whole share capital of the operating company was purchased by the Maidstone & District Motor Services Ltd., which had operated long distance services into Hastings for many years and had just taken over the local services of Messrs.Timpsons. The trolleybuses were repainted green and cream and the fleetname Hastings Tramways replaced the previous Hastings & District, a somewhat odd title since the trams had long departed. The independent power station at Parker Road, Ore, was closed in 1936 and current drawn thereafter from the municipal supply.

The year 1939 saw an order placed for 48 new double deck trolleybuses of which the first 20 entered service from 1st June 1940. The registrations (BDY 776 -823) were reserved but the war delayed delivery of more vehicles and these were eventually received in 1946 (BDY 796 -805) and 1947-48 (BDY 806 - 820). The final three registrations were surrendered and eventually appeared on lorries owned by J.Carter, a local haulage contractor. The war had brought a marked reduction in services and many of the single deck vehicles were sold, a few only remaining in use afterwards. The route structure was also in excess of the reduced demand and was simplified so that by 1945, only route numbers 1,2,3,5,6,9 and 11 were in use. 1,3 and 9 soon disappeared and 5 was renumbered 8 in 1950, leaving four routes to remain until the end of the system. These were as follows:

2   Circular. Silverhill - Bohemia - Memorial - Fishmarket - Old London Road - Ore - St.Helens - Baldslow - Silverhill.
6   Hollington - Bohemia - Memorial - Queen's Road - Mount Pleasant - Ore - St.Helens.
8   Alexandra Park - Memorial - Seafront - West Marina - Bull Inn - Bexhill - Cooden Beach.
11   Hollington - London Road - Seafront -Memorial - Fishmarket - Clive Vale - Ore - St.Helens.

In Summer an additional service, without a number, ran between Fishmarket and West Marina.

The services were efficient, cheap and reliable and the trolleybuses were well liked by the citizens. However, one problem lay behind the scenes. Legislation gave the Corporation of Hastings the right to purchase the system at five yearly intervals and the 30th June 1955 was one

such date. Although purchase was not undertaken at that time, the public interest had been very considerable and very pro-trolleybus. The next option would occur in 1960 but Maidstone & District forestalled this by seeking to wind up the Hastings Tramways Company. A strong "Save our Trolleys" campaign was waged and on 24th November 1956, the Hastings Observer editorial demanded that, "the Council, as elected representatives of the townspeople, put forward the desire for retention of the trolleybuses with all possible strength."

It was to no avail, however, and the Hastings Tramways Company ceased to exist from 1st October, 1957. The trolleybuses thereafter carried the M & D scroll but their days were numbered and in August 1958 it was announced that they would be replaced in the following year by new Atlantean buses. On the night of 31st May 1959, Sunbeam 28 worked the final journey into Silverhill depot. The next day, a ceremonial run took place from Bexhill to Hastings and the much admired system ceased to exist.

Map of services December 1935

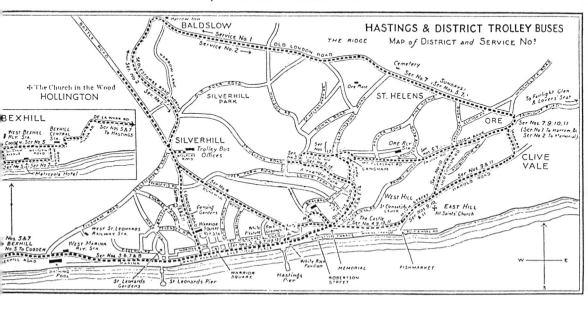

OPENING DAY

1. The inaugural run was on 1st April 1928. The day would appear to have been cold and showery but the weather has not dampened the enthusiasm of the invited guests, many of whom were ex-servicemen, or of the crews waiting to launch the new form of transport. Four open top vehicles (1 - 4) were decorated with flags, laurel leaves and daffodils. Trolleys 1, 3 and 4 are visible here and will soon join their sisters on route 4, operating between Hollington and the Fishmarket. The location is London Road, Silverhill, opposite St.Matthew's Church.
(Hastings Tramways)

MEMORIAL CLOCK
TOWER

2. The central point of the system was the Memorial Clock Tower, erected by public subscription in 1862 in memory of Prince Albert. The Clock Tower also provided a drinking fountain and remained as the centre piece of the town until, following a fire, it was wantonly destroyed by town planners in 1973. Here we see a rear view of Guy single deck 14, heading for Ore whilst 29 is bound for Hollington on route 4. The ruins of the Norman castle can be seen on West Hill, just to the right of the Memorial. (L.W.Rowe Coll.)

3. Facing in the opposite direction to the last scene, open top 2 is heading for Cambridge Road, again on route 4 to Hollington. Single deck 13 is bound for the Fishmarket on route 1. Note that the policeman is in the same position as he was in the previous view and also the time-keeper's kiosk at the junction of Cambridge Road and Robertson Street. The tram track is still in situ and the view probably dates from 1930. (Hastings Tramways)

4. By way of contrast we see the Memorial again in the last days of trolleybus operation. No.19 is in the same location as 2 in the previous picture and is also heading for Hollington. Ownership is now clearly with Maidstone & District Motor Services and the word TOWN has been added above the route number. Traffic has increased and a Leyland Royal Tiger coach is heading for the Coach Station in Queen's Road, closely followed by DH479, an AEC Regent V, working in from Eastbourne on route 15. (R.F.Mack)

5. For our last look at the Memorial we return to the immediate postwar period. No.54 was one of the few single deckers to operate after the war and is closely pursued by an AEC Regal of 1947 vintage working on route 74 to Priory Avenue. Note the belt and buckle around the fleet number on the trolleybus, as well as the bamboo pole carried above the door. This vehicle was eventually sold in September 1949. (D.C.Padgham Coll.)

MEMORIAL TO SILVERHILL

Service No. 2.   Circular Route

Via Fishmarket, Old London Road, Ore, St. Helens, Baldslow, Silverhill and Bohemia Road.

Stage No.												
I												HASTINGS (MEMORIAL).—I
28	I											Fishmarket.—28
27	I	I										Top of High Street.—27
26	2	I	I									Robertson's Hill.—26
25	2	I	I	I								Mount Road.—25
24	3	2	2	I	I							Ore (Christ Ch., Red Lake or Winch'sea Rd.)—24
23	4	3	3	2	2	I						St. Helens.—23
9	5	4	4	3	3	2	I					Hillside Road.—9
8	6	5	5	4	4	3	2	I				Harrow Inn.—8
7	7	6	6	5	5	4	3	2	I			Upper Church Road.—7
6	8	7	7	6	6	5	4	3	2	I		SILVERHILL.—6
5	9	8	8	7	7	6	5	4	3	2	I	St. Paul's Rd. (St. Peter's Ch).—5
4	9	8	8	7	7	6	5	4	3	2	I	I	Magdalen Rd.—4
2	9	9	9	8	8	7	6	5	4	3	2	I	I	Roy. East Sus. Hosp.—2
I	9	9	9	8	8	7	6	5	4	3	2	I	I	I	HASTINGS MEMORIAL.—I
28	-	-	-	-	-	-	-	-	-	-	-	-	I	I	FISHMARKET —28

Service No. 5.

Cooden, Bexhill and Hastings (Park Cross Road)

Via West Marina, Front and Queen's Road.

Stage No.													
19												COODEN.—19
18	I											Beaulieu Rd (East End).—18
17	I	I										Pages Lane.—17
16	2	I	I									Richmond Avenue.—16
15	2	I	I	I								Richmond Road.—15
14	2	2	2	I	I							Bexhill, Sackville Rd. or Hotel Metropole.—14
12	3	2	2	I	I	I						Bexhill (Central Station).—12
11	3	3	2	2	I	I	I					Dorset Road.—11
10	4	3	3	2	2	2	I	I				Penland Road.—10
9	4	4	3	3	3	2	2	I	I			Glyne Gap (De La Warr Road).—9
8	5	4	4	3	3	3	2	2	I	I		Bull Inn.—8
7	5	5	4	4	4	3	3	2	2	I	I	Bradford's Laundry.—7
6	6	5	5	4	4	4	3	3	2	2	I	I	Filsham Road.—6
5	6	6	5	5	5	4	4	3	3	2	2	I	I	West Marina (Bopeep Htl.).—5
4	7	6	6	5	5	5	4	4	3	3	2	2	I	I	Palace Pier (St. Leonards).—4
3	7	7	6	6	6	5	5	4	4	3	3	2	2	I	I	Grand Parade (Lon. Rd.).—3
2	8	8	7	7	6	6	5	5	4	4	3	3	2	2	I	Hastings Pier.—2
I	8	8	7	7	7	6	6	5	5	4	4	3	3	2	2	I	I	HASTINGS (MEMORIAL)—I
29	9	9	8	8	8	7	7	6	6	5	5	4	4	3	3	2	I	I	Alex. Pk. (Main Gates).—29
28	9	9	8	8	8	7	7	6	6	5	5	4	4	3	3	2	2	I	I	HASTINGS (Park Cross Road).—28

RETURN FARES

Stage No.		
I	HASTINGS (Memorial)	
14	Sackville Rd. or Hotel Metropole	10d.
19	Cooden	... ... 1/2
3	GRAND PARADE (London Road)	
19	Cooden	... ... 1/0

6. Leaving the town centre we follow the route via Bohemia to Silverhill and Hollington. Sunbeam 28 heads up Cambridge Road, past the steps leading down to Holy Trinity Church and the seafront. The Memorial is at the bottom of the hill. The date is 12th July 1958. (L.W.Rowe)

Service No. 6.
Hollington and St. Helens
Via Silverhill, Bohemia Road, Mount Pleasant & Ore.

```
Stage
No.
  7  HOLLINGTON.—7
  6  I  Silverhill.—6
  5  2  I  St. Paul's Rd. (St. Peter's Church).—5
  4  2  I  I  Magdalen Road.—4
  2  3  2  I  I  Royal East Sussex Hospital.—2
  I  3  2  I  I  I  HASTINGS (MEMORIAL).—I
 29  4  3  2  2  I  I  Alexandra Park (Main Gates).—29
 28  4  3  2  2  2  I  I  Langham Hotel.—28
 27  5  4  3  3  2  2  I  I  Mount Pleasant Schools.—27
 26  5  4  3  3  3  2  2  I  I  Halton Place.—26
 25  5  4  3  3  3  2  2  I  I  I  Mount Road.—25
 24  6  5  4  4  4  3  3  2  2  I  I  Ore (Christ Church, Red Lake
                                        or Winchelsea Road).—24
 23  7  6  5  5  5  4  4  3  3  2  2  I  ST. HELENS.—23
```

Service No. II.
Hollington and St. Helens
Via Silverhill, London Rd., Front, Fishmarket, Clive Vale & Ore.

```
  7  HOLLINGTON.—7
  6  I  Silverhill.—6
  5  2  I  Tower Road.—5
  4  2  I  I  Anglesea Terrace.—4
  3  3  2  I  I  Grand Parade (London Road).—3
  2  4  3  2  2  I  Hastings Pier.—2
  I  4  3  2  2  I  I  HASTINGS (MEMORIAL).—I
 28  5  4  3  3  2  I  I  Fishmarket.—28
 27  5  4  3  3  2  2  I  I  Top of High Street.—27
 26  6  5  4  4  3  2  2  I  I  Githa Road.—26
 25  6  5  4  4  3  2  2  I  I  I  Pinders Road.—25
 24  7  6  5  5  4  3  3  2  2  I  I  Ore (Christ Church, Red Lake
                                        or Winchelsea Road).—24
 23  8  7  6  6  5  4  4  3  3  2  2  I  ST. HELENS.—23
```

CHILDREN'S FARES.
Up to Three years of age, carried free. Over Three years and up to Fourteen years at the following reduced rates, with a minimum charge of Id. The child need not be accompanied by an adult.

Adult Fare	...	...	Id.	2d.	3d.	4d.	5d.	6d.	7d.	8d. 9d.
Children's Fare	...	Id.	Id.	I½d.	2d.	3d.	3d.	4d.	4d.	5d.

EARLY MORNING RETURN TICKETS.
Return Tickets will be issued at single fare rates, only on Buses due to arrive before and up to 8.30 a.m. at Memorial Hastings or any terminus. Ticket is non-transferable and available for return at any time during day of issue only.

Fare charts from the July 1949 timetable

7. At the top of Cambridge Road, 18 passes the East Sussex Hospital, replaced in 1992 by the new Conquest Hospital, located on The Ridge. The smart condition of trolleybuses in Hastings is clearly demonstrated, this scene being taken on 27th September 1958, when the vehicle was 18 years old. (L.W.Rowe)

8. Trolley 19 once again on route 6, heading towards the town centre opposite the Wheatsheaf public house in Bohemia Road on 26th July 1958. As in the last scene, people are still encouraged to visit Eire by means of the Maidstone & District programme of summer coach tours. (L.W.Rowe)

→

9. Silverhill was the site of the depot and was also a terminal for short workings on the Hollington route, as well as a layover point for vehicles on the long Circular route. This latter service heads away to the right along Sedlescombe Road North, behind trolleybus 24. The wires on the left side lead to Hollington and those to the right, immediately in front of 24, serve Beaufort Road and the depot. Two vehicles were allocated to Circular Route 2 and both are visible, taking a short layover. Note the complex overhead wiring at this busy junction. (D.A.Thompson)

→

10. AEC 7 awaits departure on route 6 from the stand used by vehicles which have ended their journey here. The Circular also used this stop when heading towards Hastings and a bamboo pole is ready to hand on the traction pole in case one vehicle needs to pass another. This is 1st February 1956 and the parade of shops can still be seen forty years on, although the types of merchandise sold have changed in the intervening years. Note that this trolleybus has a green roof and both "sunshine" and raised numerals. (L.W.Rowe)

11. We now make a short diversion to visit the depot in Beaufort Road. No.30 is facing down the road towards the depot, with the Silverhill turning circle just to the right behind the trolleybus. Note the pristine condition of the vehicle; the plate in the nearside window reads ON TEST. (L.W.Rowe Coll.)

12. Beaufort Road once again, this time heading for Silverhill. The depot lies on the left hand side of the road beyond the trolleybus, which is entering service on route 11. Note the crew walking to the depot and also the one time gas lamp, now converted to electric operation. (J.Fozard)

SILVERHILL DEPOT

13. Silverhill Depot on 14th September 1958. Note the tram tracks still in place after 30 years of trolleybus operation. On the left 40, 6 and 11 have already been withdrawn and a similar fate has befallen 45, 29 and 30 on the extreme right. At this time some vehicles of each batch had been withdrawn from service to provide spare parts to keep the rest in operation until May 1959. Vehicles 18 and 35, seen in the middle are luckier and will continue in use for a few more months. In earlier years trolleybuses had traversed the depot in the opposite direction. (L.W.Rowe)

14. Inside the depot on the same day, AEC 20 stands alongside Sunbeam 36. An enthusiasts' tour is in progress. Note the depot clock, ladders and work bench by the left hand wall. Note also that the AEC plate on 20, which in common with many others in the fleet, has lasted with the vehicle since it was new in 1940. (L.W. Rowe)

15. The exit at the far end of the depot with 40 proudly displaying crowns in each cab window. The date is 31st May 1953, just prior to the Coronation of Queen Elizabeth II. The front of withdrawn single deck 49 can just be seen; this vehicle survived until December 1955 when it was broken up for scrap. (J.H. Meredith)

HOLLINGTON

16. From Silverhill, Battle Road heads out through Hollington towards the most famous site in English history, some five miles away. The trolleybuses traversed the length of Hollington and this scene shows 10 near Paignton Road, climbing up the hill towards Silverhill. Hollington is practically devoid of traffic, although a Maidstone & District bus, perhaps on the long route 5 from Gillingham, is visible in the distance. (R.F.Mack)

11 Em 1403

HASTINGS TRAMWAYS
COMPANY

SINGLE

Passengers are requested to
see that this ticket shows
the amount of the fare paid
to the Conductor.
This ticket is issued subject to
the Rules and Regulations of
the Company and must be
shown on demand.

| DATE | MONTH | TRIP | STAGE | SHIL'GS | PENCE |

Bell Punch Company, London

11 Sk 3209

HASTINGS TRAMWAYS
COMPANY

SINGLE

Passengers are requested to
see that this ticket shows
the amount of the fare paid
to the Conductor
This ticket is issued subject to
the Rules and Regulations of
the Company and must be
shown on demand.

| DATE | MONTH | TRIP | STAGE | SHIL'GS | PENCE |

Bell Punch Company, London

17. This scene in Battle Road, at the junction of Old Church and Upper Church Roads, also shows a village without traffic, although this time the view dates from the early 1930s. A Guy open top trolleybus on route 4 pursues a lone cyclist as it commences the climb to Hollington terminus. When the system opened, a section of single line wiring existed from the village centre as far as Upper Church Road.
(D.C.Padgham Coll.)

18. The wires ended for many years at the Victoria Inn and single deck 39 is about to reverse across Battle Road before resuming the journey on route 3 to Alexandra Park. The slip board still needs changing as route 3 would not take the vehicle past the Fishmarket or Clive Vale. Note the chocolate machine and period advertisements outside the corner shop, also the Hackney Carriage plate above the registration number, quoting 32 as the seating capacity. (L.W.Rowe Coll.)

19. A wartime scene showing AEC 2 on the reversing triangle outside the Victoria Inn. Note the white markings on the wheel surrounds and on the pole in the rear. A typical M & D timetable frame can be seen on the right, whilst a passenger boards and the conductress has a chat with the driver. Photographs of double deck trolleybuses on routes 3 and 9 are rare, as the vehicles were not delivered until 1940 and the use of these route numbers was discontinued in 1946. (D.C.Padgham Coll.)

20. The same location in the period between 1935 and 1940. Guy 8 is attended by a very smart conductor, John Doyle, complete with Setright insert ticket machine and leather cash bag. Note the position of the destination box and the shape of the gantry supporting the trolley booms; these are different from the vehicles seen in the opening procession. The gantry modification was a later replacement to a stronger design. (L.W.Rowe Coll.)

→

21. The reverser was removed in 1947 because increasing traffic on the main road to Battle made the manoeuvre extremely dangerous. A new turning loop was constructed 300 yards beyond the Victoria Inn. Here 13 approaches the same stop as that used by the single decker on route 3 but the date is now 4th April 1958. Borgeauds cake shop was a useful port of call in the event of hunger striking a trolleybus crew. In the distance can be seen DH118, a rebodied Bristol K6A of M & D bound for Gravesend on the long distance route 57 which joined the Sussex coast to the River Thames in North Kent. (L.W.Rowe)

→

22. Our final call in Hollington shows the new turning circle at the Pay Gate, constructed in 1947. Trolley 23 waits to return to Ore on route 6 via Bohemia Road, Memorial and Mount Pleasant. The wires on this short section were erected two feet/610mm apart although the rest of the system used eighteen inches/457mm as standard. (D.C.Padgham)

SILVERHILL TO
ST.HELENS
(via BALDSLOW)

23. Leaving via Sedlescombe Road North, we soon reach The Briars, where 45 is seen heading for Silverhill. To the right the road leads down to the Alexandra Park terminus but this section was covered by the second circular service in Hastings, bus route 76, and was never fitted with trolleybus wiring. (L.W.Rowe)

24. The route now becomes very rural and we have reached the point where the road to Sedlescombe and Westfield continues into the distance, whilst the trolleybuses turn left to join The Ridge and then cross the bridge to call at the Harrow Inn, Baldslow. Trolleybus 26 is heading for Silverhill and is about to join Sedlescombe Road North, the main A21 road from London to Hastings. Traffic in the mid 1950s was not exactly heavy! (D.C. Padgham Coll.)

25. Sunbeam 21 has crossed the bridge and is approaching the stop outside the Harrow Inn before continuing on to St.Helens. The 21 - 30 batch of Sunbeams with 85 hp motors were regular performers on the quiet Circular Route. The trolleybus has few, if any, passengers so nobody is likely to alight here to have tea with Hovis. (D.A.Thompson)

CIRCULAR ROUTE

Via BOHEMIA ROAD, FISHMARKET, OLD LONDON ROAD, ORE, ST. HELENS & BALDSLOW

WEEKDAYS AND SUNDAYS.

	Morning																Afternoon						
	NSu	NSu	NSu	NSSu	NSu											S			NSSu			S	
				•												†			†			†	
Silverhill	6 12	6 57	7 42	8 4	8 27	9 12	9 57	1042	1127	1212	1257	142	227	2 40	312	357	4		4 44	2 4	52	527
MEMORIAL	6 22	7 7	7 52	8 16	8 37	922	10 7	1052	1137	1222	1 7	152	237	2 50	322	4	7 4		4 45	2 5	2	537
Fishmarket	6 26	7 11	7 56	8 20	8 41	926	1011	1056	1141	1226	1 11	156	241	....	326	411	....		....	456	....	541
Ore ...	6 35	7 20	8 5	8 30	8 50	935	1020	11 5	1150	1235	1 20	2 5	250	3	435	420	4		28 5	5 5	16	550
St. Helens	6 39	7 24	8 9	8 34	8 54	939	1024	11 9	1154	1239	1 24	2 9	254	3	8 339	424	4		32 5	9 5	20	554
Harrow	6 47	7 32	8 17	8 42	9 2	947	1032	1117	12 2	1247	1 32	217	3 2	3 16	347	432	4		40 5	17 5	28	6 2
Silverhill	6 55	7 40	8 25	8 50	9 10	955	1040	1125	1210	1255	1 40	225	310	3 24	355	440	4		48 5	25 5	36	610

	Evening							NSu					Morning					
				•					† ‡					NSu	NSu	NSu	NSu	NSu	
Silverhill	612	657	742	8 4	827	9 12	9 57	1022	1050		Silverhill	6 12	6 57	7 42	8 25	8 27	9 12	9 57
MEMORIAL	622	7 7	752	816	837	9 22	10 7	1032	11 0		Harrow	6 20	7 5	7 50	8 33	8 35	9 20	10 5
Fishmarket	626	711	756	820	841	9 26	1011	....	....		St. Helens	6 28	7 13	7 58	8 43	8 43	9 28	1013
Ore ...	635	720	8 5	830	850	9 35	1020	1046	1114		Ore ...	6 32	7 17	8 2	8 47	8 47	9 32	1017
St. Helens	639	724	8 9	834	854	9 39	1024	1050	1118		Fishmarket	6 41	7 26	8 11	8 57	8 56	9 41	1026
Harrow	647	732	817	842	9 2	9 47	1032	1058	1126		MEMORIAL	6 45	7 30	8 15	9 1	9 0	9 45	1030
Silverhill	655	740	825	850	910	9 55	1040	11 6	1134		Silverhill	6 55	7 40	8 25	9 13	9 10	9 55	1040

	Morn	Afternoon										NSSu								Evening			
					S					S		†											
Silverhill	....	1042	1127	1212	1257	1 42	1 53	2 27	3 12	3 41	3 57	4 5	4 42	5 27	6 12	6 57	7 42	827	912	9 57
Harrow	....	1050	1135	1220	1 5	1 50	2 1	2 35	3 20	3 49	4 5	4 13	4 50	5 35	6 20	7 5	7 50	835	920	10 5
St. Helens	....	1058	1143	1228	1 13	1 58	2 9	2 43	3 28	3 57	4 13	4 21	4 58	5 43	6 28	7 13	7 58	843	928	1013
Ore ...	....	11 2	1147	1232	1 17	2 2	2 13	2 47	3 32	4 1	4 17	4 25	5 2	5 47	6 32	7 17	8 2	847	932	1017
Fishmarket	....	1111	1156	1241	1 26	2 11	....	2 56	3 41	....	4 26	....	5 11	5 56	6 41	7 26	8 11	856	941	1026
MEMORIAL	1115	12 0	1245	1 30	2 15	2 27	3 0	3 45	4 15	4 30	4 39	5 15	6 0	6 45	7 30	8 15	9 0	945	.030
Silverhill	1125	1210	1255	1 40	2 25	2 37	3 10	3 55	4 25	4 40	4 49	5 25	6 10	6 55	7 40	8 25	910	955	1040

•—Service 11 via London Road & Clive Vale.   †—Service 6 via Mount Pleasant
‡ Service 6 via Mount Pleasant.   NSu—Not Sundays.   NSSu—Not Saturdays or Sundays
Operates until 27th September, 1955   S—Saturdays only.

Extract from September 1955 timetable

POOR ITV RECEPTION?
SOUTHERN TELEVISION

CIRCULAR
VIA
BOHEMIA. MEMORIAL
OLD LONDON RD. ST.HELENS
2

POOR ITV RECEPTION?
SOUTHERN TELEVISION

4
BDY 779

27. On the last day the Circular was operated, very unusually, by two AEC vehicles. Approaching The Harrow Inn from the St.Helens' direction is 4, closely followed by one of the few vehicles on the road. This wooded landscape further illustrates the country nature of Circular Route 2. Indeed when the system opened, single wiring was in use on The Ridge. (L.W.Rowe)

26. A few yards on from the previous scene and AEC 14 passes the sign marking the location of this peaceful country inn. This is the final day of trolleybus operation, 31st May 1959, but time appears to have stood still in Baldslow as the location continues to show a marked lack of traffic and people. (C.Carter)

28. A short distance behind the trolleybus in the last photograph and we see 4 once again on another circuit. The sylvan scene typifies the English countryside one afternoon before the building boom of the 1960s. The countryside here is now covered by the Conquest Hospital and is no longer the location for a quiet rural ramble. (C.Carter)

29. A last view of 4 on the freehold section of the Circular on the final day of operation. The photograph is taken at Grange Road on The Ridge, a location of special significance to your author, who was born in the house, seen here as McKinley's shop, on the immediate left side of the picture! (C.Carter)

30. The bend by the Parish Church of St.Helen, Ore, marks the approach to the cemetery gates and to the point where route 2 rejoins the rest of the system. Sunbeam 22 heads for St.Helens on 24th May 1958. The present church building dates from 1869.
(L.W.Rowe)

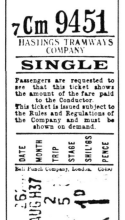

31. St.Helens Cemetery marked the eastern end of routes from Hollington and Silverhill, latterly the 6 and 11.The turning circle was in front of the gates and AEC 15 is seen here on 16th August 1958 before returning to Hollington. (L.W.Rowe)

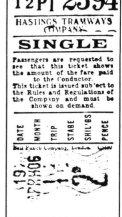

32. A spot of bother at the same location as Sunbeam 39 dewires whilst turning on the last day of operation. The wires to the left lead from the Circular and the trolleybus in the background is waiting on the stand near, very appropriately for the location, the premises of a monumental mason. (L.W.Rowe)

33. Sunbeam 30 rests by the refreshing waters available from a Metropolitan Drinking Fountain & Cattle Trough Association installation at St.Helens. To the right Elphinstone Road leads steeply downhill towards Alexandra Park and was served by bus route 75 to the Memorial and Crowhurst. This route was a regular haunt of Maidstone & District's Leyland TD5 open top double deckers. The date is 20th September 1957. (L.W.Rowe)

34. On 22nd March 1958 the road is once again completely devoid of traffic as AEC 6 awaits departure for Silverhill at the St.Helens terminus. (L.W.Rowe)

35. AEC 16 passes the site of Coghurst Hall, between St.Helens and Ore, hotly pursued by the infrequent Circular. The stop sign carries the traditional wording OMNIBUSES STOP BY REQUEST, once so typical of operations in the M & D area. Note that 16 has raised numerals on both front and cab sides and has lost the decorative AEC badge still carried by many vehicles right to the end of operations. The date is 26th May 1958. (L.W.Rowe)

36. The wires from St.Helens reached the Ore terminus at the junction with Red Lake Road, which leads away to the right and was followed by bus route 27 which terminated at the Kings Head. This photograph, taken from the upper deck of the open top trolleybus, clearly shows the wiring of the Ore terminal loop, about to be crossed by 27 on 14th September 1958. Note the array of street furniture including a Belisha beacon, a section box to feed current to the overhead and assorted lighting poles. (L.W.Rowe)

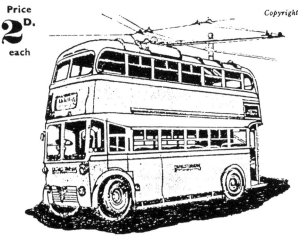

The
HASTINGS TRAMWAYS
— COMPANY —

**Associated with the British Electric Traction
Company, Ltd., and British Railways**

TIME TABLE

Commencing
WEDNESDAY, 9th JUNE, 1948
and until further notice

Price

2D.

each

Copyright

Head Office: PERCY E. GRAEFE, *General Manager.*
KNIGHTRIDER HOUSE, KNIGHTRIDER STREET, MAIDSTONE.
Phone: 2211 (7 lines)   *Grams : SERVICES, MAIDSTONE.*

37. Ore, Red Lake, and Sunbeam 38 makes the turn on route 6 as the conductor operates the frog. The road to the left continues on to St.Helens. (D.C.Padgham)

→

38. AEC 8 has completed the turn at Ore and stands ready to return to Silverhill via Mount Pleasant, Memorial and Bohemia Road on route 6. Note the overhead wiring, which allows a through trolleybus from St.Helens to overtake one that has terminated at Ore. (H.Taylor Coll.)

Front and rear covers of June 1948 timetable

39. The site of the Dog Show is not specified as AEC 14 speeds away from Ore terminus on 16th August 1958. Once again the vehicle is well turned out despite the fact that less than a year remains for the trolleybus system. (L.W.Rowe)

OLD LONDON ROAD

40. We now follow Old London Road, served by routes 2 and 6 in the latter years of the system. Sunbeam 25 is at Mount Road on 17th April 1955 and is heading for the Fishmarket on the Circular route. (L.W.Rowe)

41. AEC 3 crosses on 26th July 1958 from Old London Road to Priory Road before descending via Mount Pleasant and the Langham to the town Centre. To the right the wires lead down to the Old Market Cross and Fishmarket and are served by the Circular route. (L.W.Rowe)

42. We make a small diversion here to include a photograph of Sunbeam 22 on the short section of Old London Road that links Mount Road with the Old Market Cross. This piece of wiring was only served by the Circular and Robertsons Hill is the location of the picture, taken on 16th August 1958. (L.W.Rowe)

43. Retracing our footsteps to Mount Road junction, we follow the route via Priory Road to Mount Pleasant and the Langham. On 26th July 1958, Sunbeam 27 breasts the hill from Mount Pleasant as it heads for Ore on route 6. The corner shop is typical of the period. (L.W.Rowe)

44. Mount Pleasant forms a steep climb out of Hastings towards Ore, as is clearly shown in this photograph of AEC 11 near the Shah Hotel; this view was also taken on 26th July 1958. (L.W.Rowe)

45. From the Langham Hotel down to Alexandra Park gates the gradient increased sharply and all trolleybuses were required by Ministry of Transport regulations to engage the coasting brake before making the descent of this section of Elphinstone Road. Here AEC 9 has passed the junction with Hughenden Place and is about to commence the descent. (L.W.Rowe)

BLACKLANDS LOOP

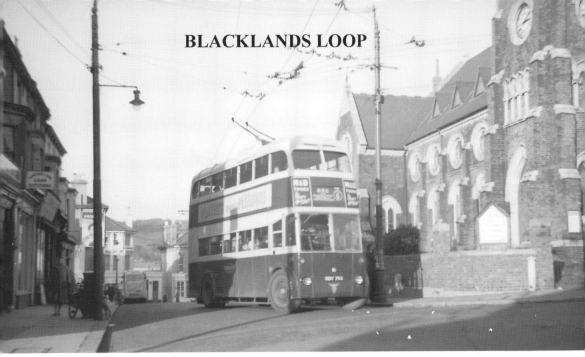

46. A turning loop existed at the Langham and was also linked to St.Helens Road by wiring via Laton Road, Blacklands Church and St.Helens Park Road, although this link had not seen regular service use since route 12 ceased in 1940. For some weeks in 1958/59, however, the link was used by trolleybuses on route 6, diverted away from Elphinstone Road due to sewer works. Here 18 rejoins Mount Pleasant and turns left towards Ore on 31st January 1959. (D.C.Padgham)

47. The other end of the loop was at St.Helens Road and 14 is shown turning from the Alexandra Park route to start the short climb to the Langham via Blacklands Church. The conductor is running across to rejoin his vehicle, having operated the frog for the turn. This section of wiring remained in place until the end, although unused apart from special workings. All this activity is taking place on 29th January 1959. (D.C.Padgham)

ALEXANDRA PARK TO MEMORIAL

48. Having travelled via Blacklands and linked up with the wires leading to Alexandra Park terminus, it is convenient here to cover this short section of the trunk route which ran from the latter terminus to Cooden Beach. The turning circle was at Park Cross Road and 41 has just completed the turn on 3rd January 1957, prior to resuming a working to Cooden on route 8. The road to the rear of the trolleybus runs alongside the park and was traversed by bus route 76; it rejoined the trolleybus wires at The Briars as seen earlier. (L.W.Rowe)

49. The junction at St.Helens Park Road was shown in photograph 47 and we now see it once again from the opposite side of the road. The park lies behind the photographer and the elegant houses behind trolleybus 33 have an excellent view from their front windows. The date is 27th September 1958 and within a year 33 will have left this peaceful scene to take up duty in the busy industrial centre of Walsall. (L.W.Rowe)

50. We have now rejoined route 6 at Alexandra Park gates, the actual junction being beyond the railway bridge, with the route to Ore proceeding to the right in front of the white painted houses. The railway line here crosses Queen's Road on the iron bridge, built in 1898 and is served by trains between Hastings and Ashford as well as electric multiple units which terminate at Ore. Trolley 17 is heading for Hollington on 20th October 1956. (L.W.Rowe)

51. This vehicle is leaving the town centre along Queen's Road. The Marks & Spencer store is still there today, although the Cricket Ground, just out of sight on the opposite side of the road, has recently been sacrificed to make way for yet another shopping mall. The unusual location of this ground gave Hastings a unique feature, which, like the loss of the Memorial, has sadly diminished the appeal of the town centre. (M & D and East Kent Bus Club)

52. Some of the busiest boarding points in the town centre were in Queen's Road and 5 is seen here picking up passengers bound for Silverhill. The Marks & Spencer store, seen in the previous photograph, is behind the lorry on the left side of the picture. This early post war scene shows an interesting collection of road vehicles, including a lady's bicycle leaned nonchalantly against the lamp-post. (L.W.Rowe Coll.)

ORE TO CLIVE VALE AND FISHMARKET

53. To complete the coverage of wiring in Hastings we now return to Ore and travel via Clive Vale and the Fishmarket to the Memorial. Here 13 turns into Saxon Road, having left the terminus at Ore. (R.F.Mack)

8Yo 8542

HASTINGS TRAMWAYS COMPANY

SINGLE

Passengers are requested to see that this ticket shows the amount of the fare paid to the Conductor. This ticket is issued subject to the Rules and Regulations of the Company and must be shown on demand.

DATE	MONTH	TRIP	STAGE	SHIL'GS	PENCE

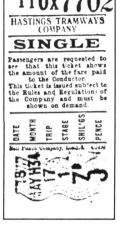

11 0x 7702

HASTINGS TRAMWAYS COMPANY

SINGLE

Passengers are requested to see that this ticket shows the amount of the fare paid to the Conductor. This ticket is issued subject to the Rules and Regulations of the Company and must be shown on demand.

DATE	MONTH	TRIP	STAGE	SHIL'GS	PENCE

54. The route via Clive Vale was flanked by residential premises and was a steady uphill climb in the direction of Ore. We witness 12 passing Godwin Road en route for St.Helens on 16th August 1958. (L.W.Rowe)

55. At the bottom of Clive Vale, above the Old Market Cross, a narrow strip of road required special traffic signals to prevent two trolleybuses passing simultaneously. The light can be seen on the standard to the right of the picture as 21 approaches the restricted section.
(D.C.Padgham)

OLD LONDON RD. HASTINGS.

56. The Old Market Cross stands at the north end of All Saints Street and is seen here in early trolleybus days with a Guy single deck vehicle on route 12 showing the destination OLD TOWN, whilst a route 1 Circular is descending Old London Road in the background.
(D.C.Padgham Coll.)

HASTINGS & DISTRICT TROLLEY BUSES.

REDUCTION IN FARES

Memorial to Mount Road and vice versa
(Only via High St. & Old London Rd.)
1D.

Fishmarket to Ore (Red Lake) and vice versa
(Only via High St. & Old London Rd.)
1D.

Offices: St. Leonards-on-Sea.
Ref. No. 17829.

W. VINCENT EDWARDS,
Engineer & General Manager.

57. At the junction of Harold Road and Old London Road the driver of no.1 pauses to check the road is clear. A sister vehicle faces the climb to Clive Vale on its way to Ore. The road layout here has been completely realigned since the demise of the trolleys. (R.J.Harley Coll.)

58. When trolleybus operation commenced, time limits were placed on vehicles passing through the narrow High Street in the Old Town and this resulted in northbound and southbound services having "time slots" during which no vehicles could run in the opposite direction. When in use northbound, southbound services from Clive Vale would be forced to reach the town centre via Old London Road, Mount Pleasant and Queen's Road, a diversion of some considerable length. The reverse would apply during times when southbound vehicles were passing. The restrictions operated only in 1929-1930 and were replaced for a short time in mid 1930 by a staff carried on the vehicles, similar to that used on single line railways. Two lines of wiring were then erected and from 10th July 1930 two way working was permitted with care at all times, although passing was still possible at certain places only. Here Guy 40 heads for St.Helens on route 10. Note the existence of three wires only, two negatives with a common positive in between; this dates the photograph as prior to July 1930. (D.C.Padgham Coll.)

59. This scene clearly demonstrates the extreme narrowness of High Street. By the 1950s the time restriction on vehicles using the road had long been discontinued but there were still only two places where trolleybuses could pass. No.38 is having no problems on the final day of operation, 31st May 1959, as it heads for the Fishmarket under the watchful eye of a young lady on the raised pavement. This charming picture, with timbered houses and small shops shows Old Hastings as it had existed for many years. Nowadays motor traffic no longer uses High Street as a through route; a new by-pass road has been constructed to the east of this location. (L.W.Rowe)

60. The area where High Street and George Street meet is known as the Fishmarket and to the east lies Rock-A-Nore and many old buildings associated with the fishing industry. A turning circle existed at the Fishmarket and was used for seafront services to West Marina and the Bull Inn, the outside wire, visible in this photograph, providing a layover facility without affecting the through trolleybuses on routes 2 and 11. AEC 9 is negotiating the circle en route for Hollington via the town centre and sea front. (D.Clark)

61. The lifeboat house is a regular feature of many seaside towns and Hastings was no exception. The doors are open for visitors, and donations to the upkeep of the lifeboat will certainly be welcomed. Above can be seen the East Hill Cliff Lift, opened in 1903 and the steepest in England with a gradient 1 in 2.8. The single deck Guy, number 33, is on route 4 and has terminated at the Fishmarket whilst a second vehicle can be seen in front of Child's Coffee House. To the rear a lorry stands beneath a sign advertising No.1 petrol, whilst the shop on the left side will develop and print your exposed film "in a few hours". (L.W.Rowe Coll.)

62. The lifeboat house can be seen again in this scene, which shows two single deck vehicles, one bound for Silverhill, passing behind the new boating pool. Before the war a mix of paddle and power boats was in evidence, although in later years only petrol driven craft were in use on the main pool. The kiosk to the right served as a pay office for the boats and the windows displayed individual boat numbers to indicate to hirers that time had run out. (L.W.Rowe Coll.)

63. The Cutter Hotel can also be seen in the previous picture, between the two single deck trolleybuses. Time has now moved on and 29 is seen at the same spot in the early 1950s on route 2. Throughout the intervening years, the hotel had remained faithful to Watneys Ales. (L.W.Rowe)

64. An early view shows Guy open top 3 in Hastings & District days on route 4 at the Fishmarket. Note the oil lamps and also the design of the upper deck guard rails. This vehicle was converted to a mobile workshop after withdrawal in 1940 but was subsequently restored to service as a decorated vehicle 3A in 1953 to mark the Coronation of Queen Elizabeth II. It became known as "Happy Harold" and survives to this day. (A.D.Packer Coll.)

FISHMARKET TO
MEMORIAL

65. We now move a few yards west alongside the
sea front and witness Guy 60 (originally 20)
passing the west end of George Street in the latter
days of single deck operation on route 2. To the
left of the Belgrave Cafe, George Street leads to
the West Hill Cliff Lift, a funicular which runs
through a tunnel formed in part from a natural
cave and which opened in 1891. The cinema
advertises talkies and the building is still there
today, although now an amusement arcade.
(C.Carter)

66. Compare the previous picture with this view of Sunbeam 31 at the same location but taken around twenty years later. It is remarkable how little has changed, even the cinema sign and the streetlamps have survived the long years of war when Hastings was in the front line of UK defences. (L.W.Rowe Coll.)

67. Looking westwards from the scene of the previous two shots, we see Caroline Parade in the early 1930s. Guy 15 is bound for Ore and is closely followed by an open top Guy on route 4, bound for the Fishmarket. The chalet and gardens, together with the road behind, have nowadays been converted to a wider road with a strictly functional car park on the seaward side. A roundabout has been provided at the road junction in the background. Hastings Pier is clearly visible in the distance. (L.W.Rowe Coll.)

68. An ominous sign for the future is the lack of parking space in this June 1955 view of Caroline Parade. However, not everyone has come in by car and trolley 24 still has a full load of locals and holidaymakers as it passes some rather elegant seafront properties. (J.H.Meredith)

69. A few yards further west and we arrive at Wellington Place where Guy 33 is on route 11 heading for Ore, whilst the cameraman is approached by a small boy with a very determined look on his face. (A.B.Cross)

HASTINGS STATION LOOP

70. Before we head for St. Leonards and Bexhill, it is convenient here to visit the Hastings Station loop. This diverged from Cambridge Road, just beyond the Post Office, and then followed Cambridge Gardens, Cornwallis Terrace and Havelock Road to return again to the Memorial. The loop was wired in one direction only and in later years saw no regular service use. In this picture, 42 is in Cornwallis Terrace on an enthusiasts' tour. (R.F.Mack)

PRIVATE

HASTINGS TRAMWAYS COMPANY

BDY 817

71. Sunbeam 45 is also in Cornwallis Terrace and stands at the terminal stop for Hastings Station, which was oddly a request rather than a compulsory one. 45 is in passenger service and working to Ore as a substitute for bus route 27 (Hastings Station to Ore) which was replaced by trolleybuses for a short time during the Suez emergency. The date is 22nd January 1957. (D.C.Padgham)

72. Looking in the other direction we see Happy Harold on a Norbury & District Model Railway Society tour on 14th September 1958. The entrance to Hastings Station is behind the wall, but the wires did not actually enter the wide and spacious forecourt in front of the station buildings. Note the word ENGAGED instead of PRIVATE on the destination blind; this was a feature of the Guy vehicles, both double and single deck. (L.W.Rowe)

73. With no regular passenger services, the station loop was a useful resting place for drivers undergoing training. No.25 is pausing in Havelock Road on 10th April 1953, before rejoining the traffic at the Memorial. (L.W.Rowe)

MEMORIAL TO SILVERHILL
(via SEAFRONT)

74. We now continue towards Grand Parade and
London Road. In the late 1930s, 5 passes through
Robertson Street bound for St.Leonards, a rather
imprecise destination for such a large area. The
vehicle has come from Ore on route 10.
(A.D.Packer Coll.)

75. A few yards further along Robertson Street and we see AEC 15 passing Trinity Street when brand new. Note the blackout masking on the headlamps as well as the white mudguards. The roof would soon be repainted green as a wartime precaution. (C. Carter)

76. At the end of Robertson Street, we join the
new promenade and 13 is seen bound for
Hollington while a few visitors are about
enjoying the air. To the left can be seen the
entrance to the new underground car park,
opened in 1931 and a far seeing piece of
construction at so early a date.
(L.W.Rowe Coll.)

77. The White Rock Pavilion, opened by the Prince of Wales on 6th April 1927, stands opposite the entrance to Hastings Pier. An open top vehicle of Hastings & District passes en route to Alexandra Park. The three wire overhead layout on the seaward side of the carriageway is a relic of the joint tram/trolleybus operation along White Rock which lasted a few months in 1928. (L.W.Rowe Coll.)

78. The road has now been resurfaced and the tramlines have disappeared. Note the very stylish ex-tramway standards on the right of the picture and the somewhat less ornate trolleybus poles outside the White Rock Pavillion. (J.H.Price Coll.)

79. Hastings was proud of its new, up to date transport system and pictures like this served to remind the public of the efficient asset the town possessed. The immaculately turned out trolleybuses are matched by the smart crews in white summer coats.   (J.H.Price Coll.)

80. Hastings Pier is clearly visible in the background as a Guy   single decker speeds towards Grand Parade. The tide is out, but few bathers are on the exposed beach. Note the small corner shop on the left side at Warrior Square gardens. (L.W.Rowe Coll.)

81. Just beyond Warrior Square Gardens we reach Grand Parade and the trolleybus has taken the inside wire before calling at the stop at the foot of London Road. The outside wire was used by vehicles continuing along the seafront, whilst route 11 turned inland. Trolleybus 23 is closely followed by an M & D double deck bus with wartime utility bodywork on 19th April 1952. (L.W.Rowe)

82. Here trolleybus 19 on route 11 is crossing the coastal wires as it swings right to begin the climb up London Road to Silverhill and Hollington. Note the seaside shelter, one of many thoughtfully provided for visitors on the sea front. (L.W.Rowe Coll.)

83. London Road links the seafront and Silverhill and passes over the railway tunnel at the west end of St.Leonards Warrior Square Station. It was served by route 11 throughout the life of the trolleybus system. Here 44 speeds down London Road, above the tunnel, on 8th April 1953. Warrior Square Station lies some distance below, to the right of the trolleybus. At the top of London Road, the wires join the Bohemia Road route just prior to reaching Silverhill. (L.W.Rowe)

GRAND PARADE TO BULVERHYTHE DEPOT

84. Returning to Grand Parade, we now head westwards towards Bexhill and Cooden. In the distance is the east end of Marine Court, a development which originally had 153 flats and three restaurants. It was designed to resemble an ocean-going liner and was constructed in 1937-38, being known locally as the Queen Mary. The Sun Terrace forms a lower promenade for people taking the sea air. A Sunbeam trolleybus bound for Cooden Beach loads passengers by the shelter and follows a Leyland single deck bus of Maidstone & District Motor Services. The small stop to the rear of the trolleybus serves the Round the Town Tour, operated at this time by Dennis Ace vehicles dating from 1938, modified to open top style. (L.W.Rowe Coll.)

85. West of Marine Court the background becomes one of seaside hotels and guest houses. Here 35 speeds along the Front on its journey to the Bull Inn. (D.Trevor Rowe)

86. The Bo-peep Hotel at West Marina is the
background to Guy 3A which has just turned on
the loop and is waiting on the inside wire to
return to the Fishmarket. The road away to the
right leads to West Marina railway station, now
long closed, whilst that immediately behind the
hotel leads up hill to West St.Leonards Station.
The date is 26th July 1958. (L.W.Rowe)

87. AEC 10 is in the process of turning on the West Marina loop having arrived from the Fishmarket on 2nd September 1952. The road to the right leads to the bathing pool, designed by Sidney Little and opened in 1933. It was a key attraction at the time the photograph was taken; the same cannot be said for the Grosvenor Restaurant, which has undoubtedly seen better days. (L.W.Rowe)

88. Beyond West Marina the wires passed under the former London Brighton and South Coast line which linked Hastings with Bexhill and Eastbourne. Sunbeam 34 has slowed to the regulation 8 mph/13 kmh in order to negotiate the bridge before passing the crossroads at the south end of Filsham Road. Note the large advertisement for the bathing pool. (L.W.Rowe)

89. The second depot on the system was at Bulverhythe and was constructed in 1906 for the opening of the tramway to Bexhill and Cooden. It later served as a base for trolleybuses on the coastal route but was closed on 30th September 1940, when wartime conditions brought about a marked reduction in services. Used as a store for redundant single deck vehicles, the depot is seen in the winter of 1940/41. Trolley 28 can be identified on the right and 56 on the centre left. As with Silverhill depot, tram tracks have survived and are clearly visible. The building still exists in 1996. (Hastings Tramways)

90. The Bull Inn was the terminus for many short workings on the coastal route and had a loop, constructed in 1947, on the seaward side of Bexhill Road. Vehicle 44 is seen taking a break before returning to Hastings. The railway line between Hastings and Bexhill is in a cutting between the trolleybus and the sea. (L.W.Rowe Coll.)

91. A short distance beyond the Bull Inn is Glyne Gap; no.43 turns from De La Warr Road on 26th July 1958. Just behind the trolleybus, the trams once took a detour on reserved track across Pebsham Marsh. A large gas works, although mercifully out of sight on the left side, still casts an ominous shadow over the scene. It was to outlast the trolleybuses by ten years, closing in 1969. (P.G.Mitchell)

92. Manor Road, Bexhill is the setting on the final evening of trolleybus operation. A few hours later Sunbeam 28 will be the very last trolleybus to carry fare paying passengers on the Hastings system. The 1946 batch of Sunbeams was rarely seen on the Bexhill and Cooden services in the later years of the system, these being the province of the 1947/48 Sunbeams with 95 hp motors; it was therefore a surprise to see 28 on Route 8 on the final day. (L.W.Rowe)

93. At the corner of Upper Sea Road a crowd waits outside the church. Was it a wedding or a jumble sale? Doubtless, the top deck passengers on 33 have a better view of events as the trolleybus snakes through the bend into Magdalen Road. (C.Carter)

94. The wires run along Endwell Road, parallel to the station platforms of Bexhill Central Station (now plain Bexhill Station), before reaching Devonshire Square where 37 is seen passing the Post Office. The footbridge on the left side crosses the railway to Station Road. (C.Carter)

95. Trouble at Devonshire Square on the Norbury & District Model Railway Society tour, seen earlier at Hastings Station. The booms are being restored to the wires with the help of one of the tour participants, whilst others look on with interest from the roadway. No doubt a glass of Guinness or Toby ale would be a welcome treat after the effort involved in getting things back to normal. (L.W.Rowe)

96. From Devonshire Square the wires diverged; a direct route to Cooden ran via Western Road and Wickham Avenue, whilst a loop served the De La Warr Pavilion via Devonshire Road, Marina and Egerton Road, then using Brockley Road to rejoin the Cooden route. Trolley 38 stands outside the De La Warr Pavilion opened in 1935 by the Duke and Duchess of York and built on the site of Martello Tower No. 47. This stop was the terminal point for journeys that did not go beyond Bexhill. (R.Cook Coll.)

97. The same view is seen some years earlier with AEC 10 on route 5. The turning circle was a few yards further on at the Metropole. After the delivery of the post war Sunbeams, AEC trolleybuses would rarely be seen in Bexhill. In the final summer of operation, the service to Bexhill from Hastings was four vehicles an hour, of these two terminated at the Metropole, one went to Cooden via Wickham Avenue and one reached Cooden via Egerton Road. (L.W.Rowe Coll.)

98. This vehicle has just made the turn from Brockley Road into Egerton Road. It is Sunbeam 34 which was saved when withdrawn from Maidstone in February 1967. Acquired by the London Trolleybus Preservation Society, it was stored at the East Anglian Transport Museum at Carlton Colville from 1974 until moved back to Hastings in September 1995. It is currently being restored by the Hastings Trolleybus Restoration Group. (L.W.Rowe Coll.)

99. The direct route to Cooden passed along
Western Road, a busy shopping street, where 39
is heading back towards Devonshire Square.
(R.F.Mack)

100. The last stretch of wiring ran along Cooden
Drive, a long, straight road which gave an
opportunity for speed. Note the line of bracket
arms which were a feature of this section of route.
Trolleybus 33 speeds along in its customary
position in the middle of the road through a scene almost totally devoid of people or traffic.
Westbound vehicles heading for Cooden Beach
found it almost impossible to pull into the kerb,
because such a manoeuvre would have risked
straying too far from the overhead, thereby
causing a dewirement. (C.Carter)

101.Cooden Beach terminus was a lonely spot. In the summer of 1939, Guy 9 waits to commence the long journey back to St.Helens whilst boats are drawn up on the shingle in the background and a lone person looks out to sea. In the early days of trolleybus operation, there was no wired circle here and vehicles turned on the shingle beach using power from a special cable linked to the lowered trolley booms and controlled by a duty pointsman. (G.E.Baddeley)

102. The same location on 14th September 1958; no.39 now occupies the stand, and car park and bus stop signs have arrived on the scene, but the location is otherwise unchanged. In the background the railway bridge can be seen adjacent to Cooden Beach Halt, whilst the Cooden Beach Hotel is just out of sight to the left. (L.W.Rowe)

ROLLING STOCK

103. The first vehicles to enter service in April 1928 were Guy BTX60s with 57 seat open top bodies by Dodson. They carried fleet numbers 1-8 (DY4953-4954, 4965-4970) and were withdrawn in 1939-1940. There were slight variations between individual vehicles during their career, particularly in regard to rear wheel covers, upper deck guardrails and the design of gantry supports. This view of 7 was taken outside Silverhill Depot and the rear wheel covers are clearly visible. (L.W.Rowe Coll.)

➤

104. The fifty Guy single deckers were 9-58, (DY5111-5140, 5452-5461 and 5576-5585). They entered service in three batches between May 1928 and June 1929 and were Guy BTX60s with 32 seat centre entrance bodywork by Ransomes, Sims and Jefferies. Most were withdrawn between 1939 and 1947 but the last remained available for service as late as 1952. Eighteen were sold for further use during the war, six each to Nottingham and Derby Corporations and six to the Mexborough & Swinton Traction Company. Trolley 34 is in Queen's Road and the white lining on the vehicle indicates a wartime scene. (L.W.Rowe Coll.)

HASTINGS TRAMWAYS Co.
OPEN TOP TROLLEYBUS

| BUILT: 1928 GUY CHASSIS | SCALE: |
| BODY: DODSON LTD. | 4mm = 1 FOOT |

DRAWING No TB 23

✳ DENOTES SLIDING WINDOW GLASSES.

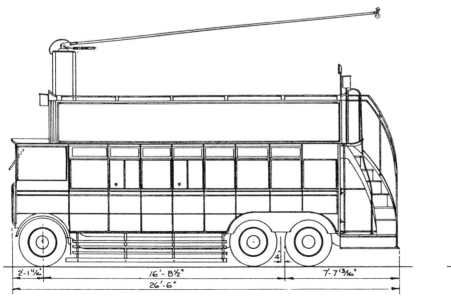

2'-1¹¹⁄₁₆"   16'-8½"   7'-7¹³⁄₁₆"
26'-6"   7'-2"

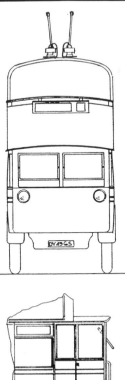

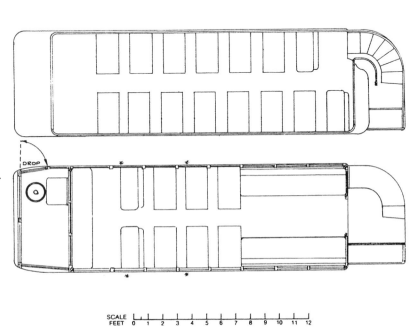

DRAWN BY:- TERRY RUSSELL, "CHACESIDE", ST.LEONARDS PARK, HORSHAM, W.SUSSEX. RH13 6EG.
SEND 3 FIRST CLASS STAMPS FOR COMPLETE LIST OF PUBLIC TRANSPORT DRAWINGS.

DROP

SCALE
FEET 0 1 2 3 4 5 6 7 8 9 10 11 12

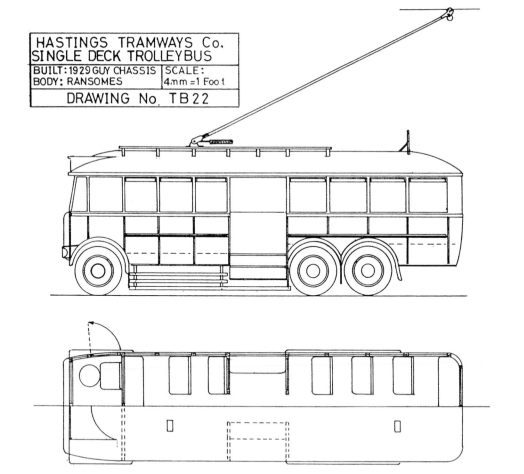

HASTINGS TRAMWAYS Co.	
SINGLE DECK TROLLEYBUS	
BUILT: 1929 GUY CHASSIS	SCALE:
BODY: RANSOMES	4mm =1 Foot
DRAWING No. TB 22	

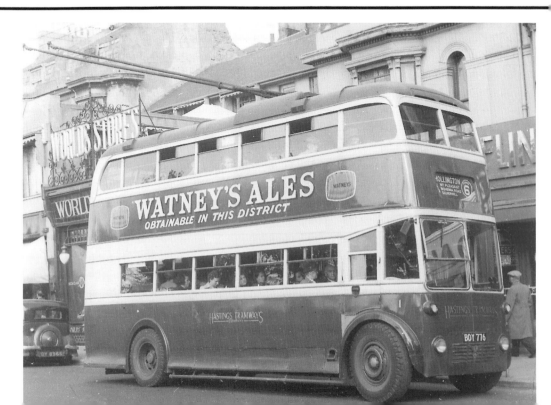

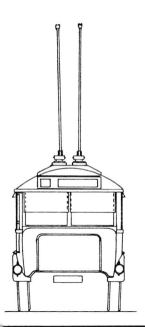

SCALE
FEET 0 1 2 3 4 5 6 7 8 9 10 11 12

WINDOWS WITH FANLIGHTS OVER
THE TOP ARE DROP LIGHTS

45

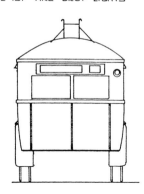

105.The twenty AEC 661T double deckers (BDY776-795) entered service in June 1940 with 54 seat bodies by Weymann (1-10) and Park Royal (11-20). All had 80 hp motors. They formed part of an initial order for forty eight vehicles, but the remaining ones were cancelled because of the war and the number received eventually totalled forty-five only. Here 1 is seen, once again in Queen's Road, Hastings. (L.W.Rowe Coll.)

106.The Park Royal batch is represented by 19, as delivered in 1940. They were virtually identical to the Weymanns. Note the wartime headlight covers, white mudguards and the Park Royal badge just *ahead of the legal ownership details, which read Percival Edmond Rudolph Graefe, Secretary, Knightrider House, Knightrider Street, Maidstone.* (Hastings Tramways)

107. After the war delivery continued of the vehicles sought originally in 1940. The next ten, 21-30 (BDY 796-805) arrived between January and April 1946 but were now Sunbeam W chassis with 56 seat bodywork by Park Royal and 85 hp motors. The batch is represented by 30, seen at Silverhill in Hastings Tramways livery. All survived the closure of the system and were then sold to Bradford Corporation for further service. (L.W.Rowe Coll.)

108. The final delivery comprised fifteen Sunbeam W chassis with 56 seat bodywork by Weymann and 95 hp motors. These were 31-45 (BDY 806-820) and were delivered between August and October 1947 (31-40) and June to October 1948 (41-45). No.32 is shown at the Queen's Road stop, again in Hastings Tramways livery. All survived to see further service in Walsall (31/3/6-9/41/4), Maidstone (32/4/5/42/3) and Bradford (40/5) after the closure of the Hastings system. (W.J.Haynes)

109. The AEC batch of double deckers had comfortable and well appointed interiors. This view shows the upper deck of No. 14, looking towards the emergency exit window at the rear. (L.W.Rowe)

110. This photograph, taken inside No.5, highlights the decorative mirrors on the front bulkhead, the neat lightbulbs and the excellent view available through the front nearside window. (L.W.Rowe)

111. When the Guy open top vehicles were withdrawn from service in 1939/40, 3 was converted to serve as a mobile emergency workshop and overhead greasing vehicle. It was transferred to service stock and numbered 3A. After the war it was stored out of use behind Bulverhythe Depot, where it is seen in this photograph, taken during a visit by the Southern Counties Touring Society. In 1953 it was restored to service in Hastings & District livery, equipped with coloured lights and went back into service to celebrate the Coronation of Her Majesty Queen Elizabeth II. In this form it survived to the end of the system and into preservation. (J.H.Meredith)

112.A number of service vehicles converted from former buses were operated during the life of the system but only two can be illustrated here. DY7860 carried the number T1 and the chassis originated from an AEC Regent delivered new to Timpsons in 1934. It received a tower wagon body from Dennis DY4846 in August 1948 and remained in use until 1956. Linesmen Field and Parry are in action on 20th April 1950. (D.C.Padgham)

113.GKE72 was formerly Chatham & District 878 and was the replacement for T1, taking the same fleet number in October 1956. It was a 1939 Bristol K5G and had originally carried Weymann bodywork. (L.W.Rowe)

114. Guy open top 3 has already been seen many times in these pages. After the system closed, it was equipped with a Commer TS3 diesel engine in 1960 and continued in use by Maidstone & District at Hastings as a unique vehicle available for carnivals and special occasions. It is now looked after by the Hastings Trolleybus Restoration Group on behalf of Hastings Council. In this photograph, it has travelled far from Hastings and is seen outside Victoria Underground Station on 21st August 1966, prior to working a tour of the Maidstone trolleybus system on behalf of the Locomotive Club of Great Britain. (L.W.Rowe)

115. Single deck Guy 45 was withdrawn (as number 46) in 1950 and in May 1953 was converted for use as a booking office for Maidstone & District coaches. It replaced an earlier single decker (22) and was placed in the Coach Station by the Cricket Ground in Queen's Road. In 1972 it was presented to the National Trolleybus Association and after storage at Pound Hill near Crawley and at Eastbourne, it is currently being restored in St.Leonards by the Hastings Trolleybus Restoration Group. It will eventually reappear as a motor vehicle to operate alongside Happy Harold. (L.W.Rowe)

FINALE
REPLACEMENT BY BUSES

116.For a short time prior to the final day, new
Atlantean buses had worked a few journeys on
the trolleybus routes to prepare drivers for the
coming changeover. For the last afternoon,
however, trolleybuses ruled supreme and here
DH495 is replaced on service 6 by Sunbeam 38
which has left the depot in Beaufort Road ready
to continue the through working to Hollington.
(L.W.Rowe)

117.The last rites were performed on Monday, 1st June 1959, when a ceremonial journey was operated from Bexhill Metropole to Hastings Memorial via the Fishmarket. Pride of place was given to Happy Harold, closely followed by Sunbeam 34 and Leyland Atlantean DH492. The assembled party of civic dignatories, company officials and invited guests pose for the scene to be recorded before departure at 11.45am. (G.E.Gregory)

CONVERSION
AT
HASTINGS

SILVERHILL
LONDON ROAD

43 DKT

This lowbridge Atlantean, seen here at Hastings, is one of 50 ordered by Maidstone and District Motor Services Ltd. who will use both lowbridge and normal height types. Forty of these buses will replace the fleet of trolley-buses at present used in the Hastings-Bexhill area. The Atlantean is a front entrance bus of integral construction with the Leyland Atlantean rear-engined chassis.

50
Atlanteans

For Maidstone and District
Motor Services Ltd.

METROPOLITAN · CAMMELL · WEYMANN LIMITED

VICKERS HOUSE, WESTMINSTER, LONDON S.W.1

118. The procession heads for Hastings along Magdalen Road, Bexhill. The Mayors have pride of place in the front seats on the upper deck of Happy Harold. On arrival at the Memorial, a luncheon will be held at the Queen's Hotel to mark the passing of the electric era and the introduction of their diesel replacements. (L.W.Rowe)

119. Happy Harold enters the depot, the very last trolleybus to operate in Hastings since it had changed places with 34 whilst at the Fishmarket. There were no crowds to witness this sad event, your author being virtually the only person there to pay his last respects. (L.W.Rowe)

120. Sunbeam 34 was not invited to stay for lunch at the Queen's Hotel and it returned empty to Silverhill after delivering the guests to the wake. It is seen entering the depot and will soon be travelling into Kent for a new life at Maidstone. Thus Hastings turned its back on a pollution free, reliable and efficient transport system. (L.W.Rowe)

Middleton Press

Easebourne Lane, Midhurst, West Sussex. GU29 9AZ Tel: 01730 813169 Fax: 01730 812601
If books are not available from your local transport stockist, order direct with cheque, Visa or Mastercard, post free UK.

BRANCH LINES
Branch Line to Allhallows
Branch Lines around Ascot
Branch Line to Ashburton
Branch Lines around Bodmin
Branch Line to Bude
Branch Lines around Canterbury
Branch Lines around Chard & Yeovil
Branch Line to Cheddar
Branch Lines around Cromer
Branch Lines to East Grinstead
Branch Lines to Effingham Junction
Branch Lines around Exmouth
Branch Line to Fairford
Branch Line to Hawkhurst
Branch Line to Hayling
Branch Lines to Horsham
Branch Line to Ilfracombe
Branch Line to Kingswear
Branch Lines to Launceston & Princetown
Branch Lines to Longmoor
Branch Line to Looe
Branch Line to Lyme Regis
Branch Lines around March
Branch Lines around Midhurst
Branch Line to Minehead
Branch Line to Moretonhampstead
Branch Lines to Newport (IOW)
Branch Line to Padstow
Branch Lines around Plymouth
Branch Line to Selsey
Branch Lines around Sheerness
Branch Line to Tenterden
Branch Lines to Torrington
Branch Lines to Tunbridge Wells
Branch Line to Upwell
Branch Lines around Weymouth
Branch Lines around Wimborne
Branch Lines around Wisbech

NARROW GAUGE BRANCH LINES
Branch Line to Lynton
Branch Lines around Portmadoc 1923-46
Branch Lines around Porthmadog 1954-94
Two-Foot Gauge Survivors

SOUTH COAST RAILWAYS
Ashford to Dover
Brighton to Eastbourne
Chichester to Portsmouth
Dover to Ramsgate
Hastings to Ashford
Portsmouth to Southampton
Southampton to Bournemouth
Worthing to Chichester

SOUTHERN MAIN LINES
Bromley South to Rochester
Charing Cross to Orpington
Crawley to Littlehampton
Dartford to Sittingbourne
East Croydon to Three Bridges
Epsom to Horsham
Exeter to Barnstaple
Exeter to Tavistock
Faversham to Dover
Haywards Heath to Seaford
London Bridge to East Croydon
Orpington to Tonbridge
Salisbury to Yeovil

Swanley to Ashford
Tavistock to Plymouth
Victoria to East Croydon
Waterloo to Windsor
Waterloo to Woking
Woking to Portsmouth
Woking to Southampton
Yeovil to Exeter

EASTERN MAIN LINES
Fenchurch Street to Barking

COUNTRY RAILWAY ROUTES
Andover to Southampton
Bournemouth to Evercreech Jn.
Burnham to Evercreech Junction
Croydon to East Grinstead
Didcot to Winchester
Fareham to Salisbury
Frome to Bristol
Guildford to Redhill
Porthmadog to Blaenau
Reading to Basingstoke
Reading to Guildford
Redhill to Ashford
Salisbury to Westbury
Stratford Upon Avon to Cheltenham
Strood to Paddock Wood
Taunton to Barnstaple
Wenford Bridge to Fowey
Westbury to Bath
Woking to Alton
Yeovil to Dorchester

GREAT RAILWAY ERAS
Ashford from Steam to Eurostar
Clapham Junction 50 years of change
Festiniog in the Fifties
Festiniog in the Sixties
Isle of Wight Lines 50 years of change
Railways to Victory 1944-46

LONDON SUBURBAN RAILWAYS
Caterham and Tattenham Corner
Charing Cross to Dartford
Clapham Jn. to Beckenham Jn.
Crystal Palace and Catford Loop
East London Line
Finsbury Park to Alexandra Palace
Holborn Viaduct to Lewisham
Kingston and Hounslow Loops
Lewisham to Dartford
Lines around Wimbledon
London Bridge to Addiscombe
North London Line
South London Line
West Croydon to Epsom
West London Line
Willesden Junction to Richmond
Wimbledon to Epsom

STEAMING THROUGH
Steaming through Cornwall
Steaming through the Isle of Wight
Steaming through Kent
Steaming through West Hants
Steaming through West Sussex

TRAMWAY CLASSICS
Aldgate & Stepney Tramways
Barnet & Finchley Tramways

Bath Tramways
Bournemouth & Poole Tramways
Brighton's Tramways
Camberwell & W.Norwood Tramways
Clapham & Streatham Tramways
Dover's Tramways
East Ham & West Ham Tramways
Edgware and Willesden Tramways
Eltham & Woolwich Tramways
Embankment & Waterloo Tramways
Enfield & Wood Green Tramways
Exeter & Taunton Tramways
Gosport & Horndean Tramways
Greenwich & Dartford Tramways
Hampstead & Highgate Tramways
Hastings Tramways
Holborn & Finsbury Tramways
Ilford & Barking Tramways
Kingston & Wimbledon Tramways
Lewisham & Catford Tramways
Liverpool Tramways 1. Eastern Routes
Liverpool Tramways 2. Southern Routes
Maidstone & Chatham Tramways
North Kent Tramways
Portsmouth's Tramways
Reading Tramways
Seaton & Eastbourne Tramways
Shepherds Bush & Uxbridge Tramways
Southampton Tramways
Southend-on-sea Tramways
Southwark & Deptford Tramways
Stamford Hill Tramways
Thanet's Tramways
Victoria & Lambeth Tramways
Waltham Cross & Edmonton Tramways
Walthamstow & Leyton Tramways
Wandsworth & Battersea Tramways

TROLLEYBUS CLASSICS
Croydon Trolleybuses
Bournemouth Trolleybuses
Hastings Trolleybuses
Maidstone Trolleybuses
Reading Trolleybuses
Woolwich & Dartford Trolleybuses

WATERWAY ALBUMS
Kent and East Sussex Waterways
London to Portsmouth Waterway
Surrey Waterways
West Sussex Waterways

MILITARY BOOKS and VIDEO
Battle over Portsmouth
Battle over Sussex 1940
Blitz over Sussex 1941-42
Bombers over Sussex 1943-45
Bognor at War
Military Defence of West Sussex
Secret Sussex Resistance
Sussex Home Guard
War on the Line
War on the Line VIDEO

OTHER BOOKS and VIDEO
Betwixt Petersfield & Midhurst
Changing Midhurst
Garraway Father & Son
Index to all Stations
South Eastern & Chatham Railways
London Chatham & Dover Railway